Let's Go To Heaven

By

David Trusty

ISBN: _ 978-1-940609-57-7 Softcover

All scripture verses are from the King James Version of the Bible
This book was printed in the United States of America.
To order additional copies of this book, contact:
David Trusty
104 Hulbert - Box 359
Alger, Ohio 45812-0359
trusty560@roadrunner.com
Or
www.Amazon.com

Published by
FWB Publications: Columbus, Ohio

FWB

Contents

Foreword

Psalm 24:3 asks, "Who shall ascend into the hill of the Lord? Or who shall stand in his holy place?" Who among men is able to stand before a just and holy God? Under what conditions is a person able to stand justified? Why do we even deserve to have this privilege? I love the answer of the Psalmist in first part of verse 4, but it also carries a heavy burden, "He that hath clean hands and a pure heart..." Although it may seem impossible, the implication which the Psalmist gives is that of possibility. This scripture speaks to the very heart of many essential doctrines, including justification and sanctification, which span 2 covenants between God and man. Just as Christ prayed for unity of his children, we are to be of one mind when discussing essential doctrine and full of grace when discussing non-essentials. My dad has explained some of the essentials. That is, how we are justified, sanctified, and more. Growing up, it was always easy to listen to him preach Biblical doctrine from the pulpit, and it was just fun listening to him explain with scripture and story the meaning behind spiritual truths to countless people. I am excited to be able to share his next book with you.

Troy E. Trusty

Introduction

Decisions

Paul writing to the church at Caesarea Philippi used these words in the first Chapter, verse twenty-three. "For I am in a strait betwixt two, having a desire to depart, and to be with Christ; which is far better: nevertheless to abide in the flesh is more needful for you." I think I understand how the Apostle felt. He is anxious to go, yet, willing to stay as long as God used him to be of some benefit to others. His decision was an easy choice due to his dedication to Christ.

I made the decision to put in print some things indwelled in my heart from the Bible.

I will be writing of several Christian doctrines which I feel will be helpful for understanding and hopefully help folks prepare and enthusiastically say, "Let's Go to Heaven".

"Oh, I wonder what they're doing up in Heaven today
Where sin and sorrow have all gone away
Where peace abounds like a river they say
Oh, I wonder what they're doing there now...."

These are a few lines from a song I heard many times in my youth without giving much thought as to any special meaning. This song was best sung by my great uncle Chalmer Howard.

As my Christian journey has been filled with many experiences that I deeply cherish in my heart I understand the best is yet to come. As I approach the end of life's journey I think more about what awaits in eternity. I think of Heaven regularly with enthusiasm, longing, and expectation.

For these reasons, I gave this book its title.

Let's Go To Heaven

Chapter 1
Why I Don't Write Fiction

Why I don't write fiction.
I seldom dream, but when I do my dreams make no sense. I am going to attempt to tell of the dream I had just last night. Really, it was this morning since I went to bed after midnight last night.

I have been a student of great American fighting men and have read about everything I find about them. George Smith Patton of WWII, has fascinated me for many years. In my dream, whenever it was, I went to listen to this great General speak. I was in full military uniform (which would not be possible since I can no longer fit into my uniform). They say, "Old soldiers never die, they just fade away". Most old soldiers and their uniforms fall into the same category as me and my uniform.

General Patton was born in 1885, died at age 60, on December 21, 1945. He was to speak November 15, 2016.

Prior to the General entering the building we were all seated. An officer came through and told all seated with our backs to the wall to remove our shoes. Like a good soldier I do as directed and remove my shoes. Then a supervisor from Wilson Sporting Goods comes by and wants my raincoat. I give it to him and he disappears from the assembly room where the dead General is going to speak. When General Patton came in to speak, and there was a huge crowd which came to hear him. He walks down the aisle by the wall I'm sitting against, stops

where I am and asks why my shoes are off. He isn't interested in all the others with their shoes off. I told him we had been ordered to remove our shoes. He said that wasn't possible and notices my raincoat isn't on. He then asks where my raincoat is. "I loaned it to a friend." He says, "No you didn't." I'm thinking, "What business is it of his? He's been dead since I was one year and two days old."

The General orders the MPs to arrest me and I ran from there, naturally without my shoes, into a warehouse. I'm looking for the supervisor at Wilson Sporting Goods and cannot locate him. Somehow, I know he can straighten this mess out. Next thing I know they have taken my Tundra, removed the wheels, had it laying across the frame of a semi with the rear tires about twenty feet from the cab. I pull the driver out of the cab, jump in, and drive off yelling "You ain't gettin' my Toyota." Instantly I am in Kenton, Ohio on ice cover streets and their city police are after me. Then I see the supervisor from Wilson Sporting Goods, rush over to him, and wake up.

What are you laughing at? I told you my dreams are always weird. This should make it obvious to everyone why I don't write fiction. My mind couldn't possibly make up something as stupid as this dream. Therefore, I will continue to write of things I know to be true with the intent of linking them to the greatest book ever written: God's Word, The Bible.

Many years ago Rev. Chad Burkhardt told of when he was a boy one of the ladies at the church he attended asked for the people to pray for her. The reason for her request was "The devil has been after me all week." Chad said he prayed saying, "Lord, don't let the devil get sister.....". He

could picture in his mind the devil chasing this poor lady all week long.

With this in mind I am made to think sometimes the sermon does not get the intended point across to the audience. So, the beginning of the next chapter will be titled: **Keep It Simple.**

Chapter 2
Explain It Simple

Explain It Simple

Some salesmen use the *KISS Formula*. "Keep it simple stupid". When you speak on a subject use words and terms that are understood by the listeners. In Sunday School one of the men said to me "You sometimes use fifteen dollar words, but you always explain the meaning of them".

In Galatians, Chapter 4, Paul used the word 'allegory'. Since it isn't a word used in every day conversations the meaning needs to be explained. An allegory is a story where the names of particular persons, places, or things have a different meaning other than face value. (My definition) The Cambridge Dictionary says "a linkstory, linkplay, linkpoem, linkpicture, or other linkwork in which the linkcharacters and linkevents linkrepresent linkparticular linkmoral, linkreligious, or linkpolitical linkqualities or linkideas."

***Explaining it Simple* - The Allegory of the Two Covenants**

My parents' generation, when correcting their children told us to "splain yourself" wanting to be told why we did or didn't do such and such. I'll do my best to "splain" Allegory in Galatians Chapter 4.

When writing about this to the church at Galatia, Paul began this Chapter mentioning the spiritual immaturity of those living under the Mosaic covenant. He mentioned the heir as a child, though he is Lord of all he is kept under supervised rule until the time appointed by his

father. This was determined by Roman law at that time. By birthright he owned the whole estate, yet he was treated somewhat like a slave in that he enjoyed no freedom and could make no decisions. The heir as a child was under guardians who watched over him, and trustees who protected his estate.

Paul used this illustration to show the contrast between the believers' previous position and what they now enjoyed. Formerly, in their state of spiritual immaturity (when we were children), they were like slaves. He described this as being under the basic principles "elements" of the world. Those who have not accepted Christ become slaves of sin.

During this time, there were legalists who wanted to insert portions of the Mosaic law into Christianity. The legalists had managed to gain the attention of many in Galatia because of their immaturity. Likely, many were novices, *newly come to the faith.*

God promised Abraham "And in thy seed shall all the nations of the earth be blessed; because thou hast obeyed my voice." These words were referring to the coming of the Messiah, the Lord Jesus Christ. When Abraham was ninety-nine years of age God appeared to him, changed his name from Abram to Abraham, his wife Sarai would now be called Sarah. The name Abraham means "father of a multitude". Sarah means "female noble, princess, queen".

Paul's motives when communicating to the Galatian Church were pure. He was aware of the desire of those who wanted to entice them to not listen to Paul's teachings so they (the Legalists) could have control over

them. In verse 19, he used the phrase ".... Until Christ be formed in you". They had drifted so far from where they were when first accepting Jesus as their Savior.
He desired they would take on the image of Christ. To be and live their lives as Jesus had. Paul's main purpose here is comparing the Mosaic Law to Grace.

We are saved by His grace through our faith in what Jesus did on the cross. Several years ago I read this acronym of Grace:

God's
Riches
At
Christ's
Expense

By our personal acceptance of Jesus Christ, we will receive God's riches, the best of Heaven and eternal life, at Christ's expense. His suffering on the cross of Calvary paid the sin debt of each person who has or ever will live. All have sinned (Romans 3:23). A prefect sacrifice was required and Jesus was the only one to qualify because He was God incarnate, God in the form of flesh.

When we accept Christ by our personal faith we become justified in the eyes of God. Often using the term 'justification' when telling people about salvation, I say "It simply means that as far as God is concerned we are: just as if we have never done anything wrong".

So now comes the part of the chapter where he uses the word *allegory*.

What he used to prove his teaching: the story of Abraham having two sons, one by the bondwoman, and the other

by the freewoman. The bondwoman was Hagar, servant to Sarah, Abraham's wife. Since Sarah had been barren she gave Her handmaid, Hagar, to Abraham so He could have a son. The greatest thing a Hebrew woman could do was give her husband a son.

Hagar gave a son, Ishmael, to Abraham. In the legal custom of that day a barren woman could give her maid to her husband as a wife, and the child born of that maid was regarded as the first wife's child. If the husband said to the slave-wife's son, "You are my son," then he was the adopted son and heir.

Gal 4:21 Tell me, ye that desire to be under the law, do ye not hear the law?
22 For it is written, that Abraham had two sons, the one by a bondmaid, the other by a freewoman.

Abraham having two sons by two women is explained. One by a bondwoman slave to Abraham's wife Sarah. The other (second) son was by the freewoman, Sarah, Abraham's wife.

23 But he who was of the bondwoman was born after the flesh; but he of the freewoman was by promise.

Ishmael, the son of the bondwoman was born after the flesh. Simply, he was born from the desire of Sarah to give her husband a son. In the first three verses of Genesis, Chapter 12, God had already promised Abraham much greatness in his seed. This causes me to feel that Sarah had too little patience to wait for God's promise to become reality. Therefore she offered her maiden to give her husband a son. This was strictly due to the desire of the flesh.

Isaac had been promised. When Sarah was 90, and Abraham 100, Isaac was born. The promise was fulfilled.

24 Which things are an allegory: for these are the two covenants; the one from the mount Sinai, which gendereth to bondage, which is Agar.

Paul explains the allegory as two covenants. Ishmael as representing the Law given to Moses on Mt Sinai, and Isaac representing Jesus Christ. Paul wrote that the Law of Moses was given as a temporary rule because men had become so wicked something was needed to fill the gap until God's promise of the Messiah would come in Jesus Christ. God promised Abraham, "in thee and in thy seed shall all families of the earth be blessed" (Gen 28:14).

25 For this Agar (Hagar) is mount Sinai in Arabia, and answereth to Jerusalem which now is, and is in bondage with her children.

Using this allegory Paul taught: the Law brought bondage and was only temporary, like the Jerusalem that existed in his day and in our day also. Flesh and blood cannot inherit the Kingdom of God (1 Corinthians 15:50). Things God intended as temporary will always be temporary.

26 But Jerusalem which is above is free, which is the mother of us all.

Revelation 3:12 and 21:2, both speak of New Jerusalem which is above, being the mother of us all. This city New Jerusalem will be permanent.

Note: the name Jerusalem means founded peaceful. The Jerusalem in Israel has seen little peace, the new Jerusalem will always be peaceful. Nothing negative will ever be there.

Many questions can be answered with a simple "yes" or "no". But occasionally we run across an individual who refuses to do so. I sometimes thought they were trying to give the impression that they were more knowledgeable than they actually are. Years ago, I asked a man a job-related question and he talked for more than ten minutes without getting near the subject I asked about.

A friend who has always been quite intelligent in high school attended a church where a well- known minister was to speak. When the service was over he told his parents that he would not be going to hear that preacher again because he needed a dictionary to understand some of the words used in the sermon. That day the sermon may have been impressive to those in academia, business owners, attorneys, etc. However, it was not simple enough for a high school honor student.

What is the result of that well-known preacher's message? A completely lost opportunity to share Christ with a very interested young man. Had he "explained it simple" the impression could have had a tremendous impact on the honor student.

Lost opportunities are so sad because they are usually lost forever. Only rarely do they come again.
While "explaining it simple", be yourself. Using one level of speaking for one group and a higher or lower level when speaking to others can cause folks to think negative about you.

You can meet and greet people on their level(s), but addressing a crowd or congregation "explain it simple" will get the point across to each person.

Apostle Paul said in *1 Cor 9:19, "For though I be free from all men, yet have I made myself servant unto all, that I might gain the more.*
20 And unto the Jews I became as a Jew, that I might gain the Jews; to them that are under the law, as under the law, that I might gain them that are under the law;
21 To them that are without law, as without law, (being not without law to God, but under the law to Christ,) that I might gain them that are without law.
22 To the weak became I as weak, that I might gain the weak: I am made all things to all men, that I might by all means save some.
23 And this I do for the gospel's sake, that I might be partaker thereof with you."

Paul was not saying that he spoke on different levels, which, I have no doubt he had the ability to do so. He was delivering the same Gospel to every person or group no matter their social, political, financial, or religious status in life.

Let all Christians submit themselves completely to God for whatever purpose He desires of us. This commitment we must make.

Chapter 3
Are You Bulletproof?

Are you bulletproof?
When I was a kid Dick Tracy of the comics had a wrist radio which I thought would be nice but also thought it to be preposterous. Cell phones today are a reality. This makes me think of the story of the Tower of Babel they tried to build to Heaven.

Gen 11:5, And the Lord came down to see the city and the tower, which the children of men builded.
6 And the Lord said, Behold, the people is one, and they have all one language; and this they begin to do: and now nothing will be restrained from them, which they have imagined to do.

Verse 6, the words "*and this they begin to do: and now nothing will be restrained from them, which they have imagined to do*", means exactly what it says. Whatever we set our minds to do is possible with enough put into it, unless God intervenes.

With all the developments in technology, including the bulletproof vest, we humans are not invulnerable. The vest protects the vital organs, leaving the head exposed. Without the brain, none of the other vital organs will function. Therefore no one is bulletproof.

All this to reach the point that all Christians are in a battle, but not with guns and other weapons of war. Our battle is against the devil and all the cunning devices he uses. Currently we live in one of the worst times in the history of Christianity. Rev. David Rowe made the

statement over forty years ago, "Christianity is one of the most abused words in our society". This statement has grown truer over the years.

Many professing Christianity fail to live up to the meaning of the word "Christian". It simply means Christ like. Jesus never cursed, told dirty jokes, lied, cheated, never gave in to temptations, and always stood for what right.

Satan tries every way possible to get Christians to sin. He uses sex, drugs, alcohol, money, and power. He knows the Bible better than many church goers, and even tried using it to deceive Jesus himself. Scripture teaches that Jesus was tempted in all points like we are yet was without sin. As humans, we have an inherited trait to do the wrong thing. Tots will do what they have been told not to do. I've seen this with our sons. They knew I saw them and I asked "Did you do ....", and they would say "No". Not a single person after accepting Christ into their life has lived a perfect live. We have each done things we should not or failed to do what we should have.

I am so thankful for what John wrote in 1 John 2:1, "*My little children, these things write I unto you, that ye sin not. And if any man sin, we have an advocate with the Father, Jesus Christ the righteous:*
2 And he is the propitiation for our sins: and not for ours only, but also for the sins of the whole world."

To have an advocate – a person who pleads the cause of another in a court of law – we then plead our case asking forgiveness.

Propitiation – that by which it becomes consistent with God's character and government to pardon and bless the sinner.

The Christian isn't perfect but we have been forgiven. To maintain that forgiveness, we must come to Jesus, ask for forgiveness. Admitting we did wrong is the beginning. 1 John 1:8, tells us: "*If we say that we have no sin, we deceive ourselves, and the truth is not in us.*
9 If we confess our sins, he is faithful and just to forgive us our sins, and to cleanse us from all unrighteousness."
These verses explain themselves.

If we say we did nothing wrong, being unwilling to admit to our sin, we are only deceiving ourselves. If we confess, admit to, our wrong, then He will forgive us and wipe the slate clean. In His eyes, we will be as though we never committed the wrong.

Chapter 4
Birth Of The Church

Birth of the Church

When many people read Acts, Chapter Two, their attention is grabbed by the events of the cloven tongues of fire sitting on the people or the speaking by the Galileans in a language they had never learned. The greatest event of this Chapter is the fact that it is the birth of the Church.

The Bible never uses the phrase "birth of the Church". Pentecost is the culmination of all events leading to the Church coming into existence. The birth, life and ministry of Jesus, His death, burial, and resurrection are events necessary before Pentecost. Jesus, after His resurrection, had instructed the disciples to tarry in Jerusalem until they would receive power (the Holy Spirit). Jesus spoke the following in John 16:7, Nevertheless I tell you the truth; It is expedient for you that I go away: for if I go not away, the Comforter will not come unto you; but if I depart, I will send him unto you.

8 And when he is come, he will reprove the world of sin, and of righteousness, and of judgment:
9 Of sin, because they believe not on me;
10 Of righteousness, because I go to my Father, and ye see me no more;
11 Of judgment, because the prince of this world is judged.
12 I have yet many things to say unto you, but ye cannot bear them now.
13 Howbeit when he, the Spirit of truth, is come, he will guide you into all truth: for he shall not speak of himself;

but whatsoever he shall hear, that shall he speak: and he will shew you things to come.

After Jesus ascended, the Holy Spirit took His place in dealing with people about their souls. Two things I should point out: The Holy Spirit is a He not an it, and the word Pentecost simply means fiftieth. The fiftieth day after Passover.

After God the Father, and God the Son had done their parts, God the Holy Spirit came to do His part until the second coming of God the Son, which will be when He comes to get His Bride, the Church.

Through knowing this we can conclude that the Church was born on the day of Pentecost. Proof of its birth is given after the sermon delivered after he stood among them to clarify that what they were witnessing was something far different than them being drunk. Peter began by explaining the Galileans who spoke were not drunk since it was only the third hour of the day. He was saying as we might today, "the bars and taverns weren't even open yet". Peter's sermon was a fantastic history lesson about the Jews and their dealings with God.

God used what Peter spoke to touch the hearts and minds of three thousand people on that day in a manner that caused them to believe what he said and call upon the name of Jesus because of their sins.

Imagine three thousand people surrendering to Christ at once. The message had to be powerfully seasoned by the Holy Spirit.

Those coming to Christ on that day was a sign that the Kingdom of God was established as well as the purpose of the Church was demonstrated. That purpose being to lead people to Jesus Christ.

The church has been through many difficult times since it was founded on that Day of Pentecost.

During the first hundred years of the church all the apostles were slain except for John, who was banished to the isle of Patmos.

- Approximately 135 A.D. many Jews were exterminated. Because of this the Jews were scattered to all nations.
- Early in the 2nd Century Martyr worship began in Rome and infant baptism was introduced.
- From 1087 to 1294, the Jews were persecuted excessively.
- In 15th Century England came a time of persecution unimaginable for a civilized nation.
- Along comes Hitler during the 1930s and 1940s.

Islam now is trying to take control of the world through methods of infiltrating countries and demand those countries adopt the Islamic culture.

When Golda Maier was Prime Minister of Israel she was asked if the Jews and Palestinians could ever co-exist peacefully. The answer she gave still rings true today. "When they learn to love their children more than they hate us." Islam thinks nothing of strapping explosives to a child and sending it on a suicide mission. Could you do that to your child?

Persecution will always exist in some form. Just remember the words of Jesus in John 16:33, *"In the world ye shall have tribulation: but be of good cheer; I have overcome the world."*

He is telling us to look ahead to our eternal reward. He overcame every temptation known to mankind, let's look to Him and we can also overcome.

Chapter 5
Sanctification

Sanctification
That which is sanctified is something set aside for a holy use. With this definition, many would think sanctification is the process or way we become sanctified.

Chapter 17, of St. John is a prayer of Jesus to God the father on behalf of not only His disciples, but for all people needing Him and His guidance on their journey through life.
Verses 17 through 19, He mentions "sanctify" concerning Himself and the disciples.
John 17:17 Sanctify them through thy truth: thy word is truth.
18 As thou hast sent me into the world, even so have I also sent them into the world.
19 And for their sakes I sanctify myself, that they also might be sanctified through the truth.

Jesus had prayed for protection for His disciples. Now His second petition for them was for their sanctification. Sanctify means "set apart for special use." Christians are to be distinct from the world's sin, its values, and its aims. In the 1980s, Dr. Melvin Worthington spoke at Ohio Free Will Baptist State Convention. He made a statement I have never forgotten. As Christians, "we are in the world, living distinctly different from the world as a testimony to the world".

The means of being sanctified is God's truth. That truth is His Word, the Bible. When the message about Jesus is

heard, believed, and understood, hearts and minds are captured. This results in a change in our thinking and attitudes thereby changing our lives. The same happened to the disciples and others who accepted Jesus while He was on earth. As they applied God's Word to their lives, they were sanctified, set apart for God.

God's message set the apostles apart from the world so that they would do His will.

Jesus sanctified Himself. Why did He need to sanctify Himself? Was He not already set apart to God and different from the world? I think this refers to His mission of going to Calvary and there paying our debt for sin which no one else could do. His purpose in life was His death. Fulfilling that purpose, He had to be sanctified to it. Set apart as a perfect sacrifice to die for us. In His death then we can be sanctified.

How long does sanctification take?

I now ask this question. The answer to this question depends upon whom you ask. Different denominations believe differently. Some believe in "two works of Grace", others in three. Those believing two are being saved and sanctified, while those believing three, *being saved, sanctified, and filled with the Holy Ghost.*

My answer to this question is based upon what the Apostle Peter wrote in 2 Peter 1:2 Grace and peace be multiplied unto you through the knowledge of God, and of Jesus our Lord,

2 Peter 3:18 But grow in grace, and in the knowledge of our Lord and Saviour Jesus Christ. To him be glory both now and forever. Amen.

Here Peter tells us of grace and peace, may it be enhanced, grow continuously; he wants us to be multiplied through the knowledge of God and of Jesus our, Lord. In vs. 18, of Chapter three, the last verse of the book, grow in grace, and in the knowledge of our Lord and Saviour Jesus Christ. The growth of each Christian is based on our knowledge of God and Christ.

Here, I admit that though I am not the sharpest knife in the drawer, I am still learning from God's Word. Therefore, I conclude that sanctification is a lifelong process. Continuous learning means continual growth. Sanctification will only be completed when we arise from the dead or are changed instantly at Jesus return. The last portion of Psalm 17:15, "... I shall be satisfied, when I awake, with thy likeness." Only then will we be completely sanctified. We will be totally set apart for God's use.

I'm sure some will disagree believing they have already been sanctified. Since early childhood I have heard many people testify in worship services, "I'm saved, sanctified, and filled with the Holy Ghost". They are speaking of three works of grace which many charismatics truly have accepted as Biblical fact. Other church organizations believe in two works of grace. I firmly believe the Bible simply teaches that we are saved by His grace, through our faith. Before expounding on this I need to throw in a new word to be considered.

That word is Hermeneutics. This is the science of interpretation. Before we accept various doctrines a thorough and in-depth study must be made. This requires using every resource available. It surprises me that such a large number of Christians are totally

unaware as to what is available. In 2016, we had a thorough study at church on spiritual gifts. The first lesson pointed out something all students of the Bible should follow. Know what the Bible is saying and never adjust God's Word to fit your experience, and never let your experience overrule God's Word. Also, common sense being applied can be enlightening at times.

Sanctification is being set apart for a holy use. Common sense tells me that we deal with everyday life, all its entanglements, we therefore cannot be fully or completely sanctified. Completeness will come when we receive our new body when Christ returns.

Chapter 12, of First Corinthians compares the spiritual gifts to the human body with the intent of showing that the gifts work together to accomplish God's will as the members (parts) of the body work together to perform its tasks. Beginning in verse 27, he tells us:
"Now ye are the body of Christ, and members in particular.
28 And God hath set some in the church, first apostles, secondarily prophets, thirdly teachers, after that miracles, then gifts of healings, helps, governments, diversities of tongues.
29 Are all apostles? are all prophets? are all teachers? are all workers of miracles?
30 Have all the gifts of healing? do all speak with tongues? do all interpret?
31 But covet earnestly the best gifts: and yet shew I unto you a more excellent way."

Explaining how God put different elements in the church, and what order, he then asks some rhetorical questions, (Questions asked that the asker is aware the one asked knows the answer).

Each question has the word all emphasized. Do all, have all are all, etc.

Using just the head of a body as to illustrate:
If I only have eyes on my head I won't live long. How am I going to eat without a mouth? If I am all ears (no pun intended) and still no mouth – the same results. All parts of the body must function together for the proper use and care of it.

The very same goes for spiritual gifts.

Are there any Apostles in the world today? I've read articles supposedly written by this apostle or seen on television another claiming to be an apostle. Are they really what they claim?

An answer to one question gives the answer. What distinguished the Apostles? Answer: They all received their commission directly from Jesus being eye witnesses of Him. Each saw Him personally. Paul saw Him on the road to Damascus after His ascending from Mount Olivet. The closer you look GREATER is His Book!

Chapter 6
Appointments

Appointments

Each of us have appointments as we go through life. Doctor appointments, due dates of bills qualify as appointments, dating the opposite sex, weddings, and many other things.

Human beings are destined for two things. Hebrews 9:27, states "*And as it is appointed unto men once to die, but after this the judgment:*
28 So Christ was once offered to bear the sins of many; and unto them that look for him shall he appear the second time without sin unto salvation."

These are appointments we all must keep. One thing stands out in my mind about these appointments. None of us know when they are scheduled.

Job 14:5 "*Seeing his days are determined, the number of his months are with thee, thou hast appointed his bounds that he cannot pass;*"

Man's life is short. His days and months are determined by God. We are hemmed in by this numbering of our days. God knows when each of us will meet death. Only He knows when Jesus will return. Upon that return the judgment must take place.

Dan 7:9, "*I beheld till the thrones were cast down, and the Ancient of days did sit, whose garment was white as snow, and the hair of his head like the pure wool: his throne was like the fiery flame, and his wheels as burning fire.*

10 A fiery stream issued and came forth from before him: thousand thousands ministered unto him, and ten thousand times ten thousand stood before him: the judgment was set, and the books were opened."

That second appointment is coming. We have been properly warned to make preparation for it. Please do so now. Before it is too late.

Chapter 7
Confidentiality - Things I Have Been Told In Confidence

Confidentiality – Things I have been told in confidence

As a preacher and Pastor I have been told many things in confidence. Some of these were heart-breaking, some humorous, and a few disturbing. Please go to the next page to find out about some of these. You may be surprised.

SURPRISE – If you were expecting to read some good ones, I apologize. I can't tell.
Things told in confidence to me I can never reveal, not even to my wife. To do so would be ethically wrong, could be embarrassing to those who had spoken to me in confidence, as well as morally wrong on my part. Occasionally I recall some of the funnier conversations; but, have never been tempted to relate anything to others.

Every Pastor or Clergyman must hold himself to that standard. Any who does not will certainly be found out and the results will ruin his reputation and possibly bring much harm to the church he is associated with. We aren't even allowed to be as the ladies from the Hee-Haw TV Show that sang "You'll never hear one of us repeating gossip, so you better be sure to listen close the first time". What could be the worst outcome, is the damage done to the person who confided in us possibly could be devastated to the point of walking away from Christianity forever.

Chapter 8
Name It And Claim It

Name It and Claim It

This phenomena has been prevalent in a large number of churches and has been accepted as one hundred percent true. I've both heard and read of people saying, "I claim victory over this", "I claim healing for so and so ...". Some have in prayer said, "God, I command you to do ....". What would make anyone ever to think they have any right or authority to give orders to their creator? This teaching truthfully distorts Biblical truths.

Some followers of this idea use different verses of the Bible out of context to try supporting their beliefs. Here are a couple examples.

Matt 18:19 Again I say unto you, That if two of you shall agree on earth as touching any thing that they shall ask, it shall be done for them of my Father which is in heaven.
Matt 21:22 And all things, whatsoever ye shall ask in prayer, believing, ye shall receive.

An individual asks for God to give him a new vehicle. He decides what he wants, goes to the dealer, makes an agreement, buys it. He gets a payment book with it. To me, that is not a gift. A gift is something without cost to you. Now, I also understand that this person when asking God for a new vehicle and claiming it may have meant in his own mind, "Lord help me to purchase and pay for it over time". However, by their claiming something makes it incongruous with the Bible. It doesn't match scripture.

I believe the above verses are concerning spiritual matters. If we ask God to deal with the heart of someone concerning their soul, and Matthew 18, is dealing with someone in the church who has done wrong and refuses to admit it or make it right, then we are all to pray for that person.

Rev. Chad Burkhardt telling of when he was a boy one of the ladies at the church he attended asked for the people to pray for her. The reason for her request was "The devil has been after me all week." Chad said he prayed saying, "Lord, don't let the devil get sister so and so". He could picture in his mind the devil chasing this poor lady all week long.

Every person in the world, especially Christians should be aware of the fact that "the devil is always after each of us". He is sly and cunning in many ways. Some of the biggest lies he tells those not saved are: "You have plenty of time." He convinces people that they have plenty of time to enjoy the pleasures if sin. You are going to live a long time and therefore, there is no need to come to Christ yet.

He has convinced many that there will not be a day of reckoning. In the end God will look at their life and if the good deeds we have done outweigh the bad things He will accept us into Heaven. Nothing could be further from Biblical teachings. Paul, the apostle, in his sermon at Mars Hill told the people of Athens of a definite God appointed time when we must answer for the way we have lived our lives.

Acts 17:31 *"Because he hath appointed a day, in the which he will judge the world in righteousness by that man whom*

he hath ordained; whereof he hath given assurance unto all men, in that he hath raised him from the dead."

What will please God on that day is our having accepted the atonement blood of Jesus Christ shed at Calvary. With this in mind, I will endeavor to share various scriptures which point to His offering of Himself for us.

John 10:11 I am the good shepherd: the good shepherd giveth his life for the sheep.
John 10:15 As the Father knoweth me, even so know I the Father: and I lay down my life for the sheep.
16 And other sheep I have, which are not of this fold: them also I must bring, and they shall hear my voice; and there shall be one fold, and one shepherd.
17 Therefore doth my Father love me, because I lay down my life, that I might take it again.
18 No man taketh it from me, but I lay it down of myself. I have power to lay it down, and I have power to take it again. This commandment have I received of my Father.
Heb 1:1 God, who at sundry times and in divers manners spake in time past unto the fathers by the prophets,
2 Hath in these last days spoken unto us by his Son, whom he hath appointed heir of all things, by whom also he made the worlds;
3 Who being the brightness of his glory, and the express image of his person, and upholding all things by the word of his power, when he had by himself purged our sins, sat down on the right hand of the Majesty on high;

In Chapter nine of the book of Hebrews the writer, assumed to be Paul, tells about the Tabernacle, the veil, and the most holy place, referred to as the Holy of Holies. Into the most holy place went only the high priest. He could enter only one time per year, on the Day of

Atonement. As he entered he was required to take sacrificial blood for his own sins as well as the sins of all the people of Israel. With the death of Jesus on the cross He became "the high priest of our profession". At His death, He entered into the most holy place with His own blood being offered for the sins of the people. There was no need for blood sprinkled for Him because He was perfect, sinless, having never done anything wrong. He lived a sinless life, being tempted as recorded in Hebrews 4:15, *For we have not an high priest which cannot be touched with the feeling of our infirmities; but was in all points tempted like as we are, yet without sin.*

Chapter 9
Justification

JUSTIFICATION

Since the Bible states that we have all sinned we have a need to be brought back into proper fellowship with God. When a person has been restored to that fellowship he or she then stands justified in the eyes of God, just as though we had never done anything wrong in our life.

Justification comes about by believing in what Jesus did at Calvary and repenting of our sins. Personally accepting after we truly realize Jesus is the sacrifice that pleased God as payment for all sins of each individual.

Hebrews 9:22 states "*And almost all things are by the law purged with blood; and without shedding of blood is no remission.*"
Acts 13:36 For David, after he had served his own generation by the will of God, fell on sleep, and was laid unto his fathers, and saw corruption: 37, But he, whom God raised again, saw no corruption.

Paul tells us David died, was buried, and his body decayed. However, Jesus died, was buried, but his body did not rot (decay).

38 Be it known unto you therefore, men and brethren, that through this man is preached unto you the forgiveness of sins: 39, And by him all that believe are justified from all things, from which ye could not be justified by the law of Moses.

Now he explains that through Jesus Christ is preached to us the forgiveness of sins, and all who believe are justified from all things. By accepting in our heart what Jesus did by his sacrifice at Calvary, which must be done in faith, believing he did it for everyone all over the world makes a person justified, to be just as though he/she has never done anything wrong. When I personally accepted by faith, Jesus sacrifice, everything I ever had done wrong, every sin I had ever committed were covered by the blood of Jesus Christ. When God looks at a Christian, He sees Jesus blood which justifies.

Rom 3:24 Being justified freely by his grace through the redemption that is in Christ Jesus:
25 Whom God hath set forth to be a propitiation through faith in his blood, to declare his righteousness for the remission of sins that are past, through the forbearance of God;

To become justified is free, because it is through the grace of God. Grace is "undeserved, unearned, unmerited favor and fellowship with God. An acronym is made by using the letters of a word to define that word. Example: I served America from July 1962, until July 1966, in the USAF, United States Air Force. Years ago I read an acronym of grace. "God's riches at Christ's expense". We obtain membership in God's family only by the price Jesus paid when he died in our place at Calvary.

Verse 25, says God made Jesus to be a propitiation, one who propitiates, one who eases the anger or dissatisfaction of another. This act being our Savior, the Lord Jesus Christ, made appeasement with God on your and my account.

26 To declare, I say, at this time his righteousness: that he might be just, and the justifier of him which believeth in Jesus. 27 Where is boasting then? It is excluded. By what law? of works? Nay: but by the law of faith. 28 Therefore we conclude that a man is justified by faith without the deeds of the law.

God's reason for the propitiatory death of Jesus was to prove to mankind that God was just, and the only justifier. Only God justifies, and only one way, the death of his Only Begotten Son. We receive this justification by our faith that all he did was for bringing man back into good standing with Himself.

Requiring the blood of a perfect sacrifice would and did bring Justification to lost and unforgiven souls.
Writing to the Hebrews, chapter nine, verse twenty-two, Paul refers to Old Testament law and to New Testament grace.
"And almost all things are by the law purged with blood; and without shedding of blood is no remission."
The words 'nearly everything' speaks of the graciousness of God under the law for the poor. Some could not offer an animal sacrifice due to poverty, but could bring a flour offering. The apostle saw the entire structures of both law and grace. Probably thinking of the Day of Atonement under the law which was a ritual for the sins of all Israel under the Covenant of the Law. He is alluding to the fact without shedding of blood no one can be forgiven, which Christ did at Calvary.
Matthew wrote of Jesus death and events occurring immediately thereupon.
Matt 27:51 And, behold, the veil of the temple was rent in twain from the top to the bottom; and the earth did quake, and the rocks rent;

52 And the graves were opened; and many bodies of the saints which slept arose,
53 And came out of the graves after his resurrection, and went into the holy city, and appeared unto many.
The veil being torn is quite significant. Torn from the top, God did it showing His role in the plan of salvation.

Torn from top to bottom, God opened salvation to all mankind.

Reason it was torn, so Jesus could enter.

Hebrews, Chapter nine explains that the veil separated the holy place from the Holiest of All.

Behind this veil only the high priest could enter, and only on the Day of Atonement. He could only enter with blood shed for his sins and the sins of the people. When the veil, which was nearly four inches thick, opened at Christ's death He entered by His own blood being shed for the people. There was no blood shed for Him because He was perfect.

The torn veil also made it possible for individuals to approach the throne of grace. At the bidding of Christ through the Holy Spirit, we are drawn to repentance and can accept Jesus personally in each of our lives.

Mark 2:7, and Luke 5:21, shares the Jewish troublemakers asking the question "Who can forgive sins, but God ...."? This was asked after accusing Jesus of blasphemy. The Jewish leaders were right that only God can forgive sins. However, they failed to realize that Jesus Christ was God incarnate, God in the flesh. Sins can only be forgiven by God the Father, God the Son, and God the

Holy Spirit. No preacher, pastor, evangelist, priest, rabbi, nor any human being can do that. Sins are forgiven by a person believing in what Jesus did by his sacrificial death at Calvary, confessing "I accept what He did for myself." Our faith comes from our heart, believing in our heart is different than believing in our mind. Consider these two verses from Job.

Job 32:7 I said, Days should speak, and multitude of years should teach wisdom.
8 But there is a spirit in man: and the inspiration of the Almighty giveth them understanding.
Verse eight is a conclusion drawn from verse seven and a few preceding verses. God placed something within each person, a spirit, with the Holy Spirit we each understand that we have a need for Jesus death in our place at Calvary.

Chapter 10
Baptism

Baptism

Let us look at Romans Chapter six. Paul opens by asking a rhetorical question (a question that the person asking it already knows the person asked knows the answer; asked to make a point). He asks if as Christians we should continue to sin so God's grace would continue to forgive us thereby His grace would grow? Should believers sin more so we can experience more grace?

"Definitely not" is his answer. How can we that died to sin when we accepted Christ continue to live a sinful life as before.

Romans 6:3 Know ye not, that so many of us as were baptized into Jesus Christ were baptized into his death?
4 Therefore we are buried with him by baptism into death: that like as Christ was raised up from the dead by the glory of the Father, even so we also should walk in newness of life.
5 For if we have been planted together in the likeness of his death, we shall be also in the likeness of his resurrection:

These verses give as clear a definition of baptism as is found in scripture.

- First, we have died to sin.
- Second, when someone dies they are buried. Since we died to sin we are to be buried.
- Third, we are buried with Him by baptism.
- Fourth, we are raised to walk in a newness of life.

Here are some definitions of bury. *to put in the ground and cover with earth:*

- *To put (a corpse) in the ground or a vault, or into the sea, often with ceremony:*
- *To cover in order to conceal from sight:*

Strong's Greek dictionary says this about baptism:
baptizó: to dip, sink
Original Word: βαπτίζω
Part of Speech: Verb
Transliteration: baptizó
Phonetic Spelling: (bap-tid'-zo)
Short Definition: I dip, submerge, baptize
Definition: lit: I dip, submerge, but specifically of ceremonial dipping; I baptize.

Baptism is only for believers. This may not be a popular statement to many people, especially those who baptize infants. I made the statement because of what baptism says. It is a public exhibition expressing our faith in Christ.

Baptism is an outward expression of an inward experience. It says "I have died to the manner of life I have been living by accepting Christ and being made a new creature in Him. The old life I have lived is over. I am buried with Christ and resurrected to walk in a newness of life." I will be living differently than I have in the past because my focus in life will be directed elsewhere. I now have one primary goal in life. That is to live a life intended to honor God and His Son.

The opening sentence of the previous paragraph that "baptism is only for believers" needs explanation. Every person John the Baptist baptized came repenting of their sins first. They were coming to John, confessing their sins and being baptized.

Matt 3:5 Then went out to him Jerusalem, and all Judaea, and all the region round about Jordan,
6 And were baptized of him in Jordan, confessing their sins.
Being aware of their sins they came to John.

In Acts 8:36 and 37, Luke writes about the evangelist Philip being sent to Gaza to explain Jesus to only one person. An Ethiopian eunuch reading from Isaiah 53, had what he was trying to understand made clear to him.
36 And as they went on their way, they came unto a certain water: and the eunuch said, See, here is water; what doth hinder me to be baptized?
37 And Philip said, If thou believest with all thine heart, thou mayest. And he answered and said, I believe that Jesus Christ is the Son of God.
He recognized his sins, believed in Jesus, confessed who Jesus was, and was then baptized.
In what is referred to as the "resurrection chapter" of the Bible, Paul wrote:
1 Cor 15:29 Else what shall they do which are baptized for the dead, if the dead rise not at all? why are they then baptized for the dead?

He most likely using this term to emphasize the resurrection of the dead because some did not believe in it. Using this phrase, I think he was informing us to make preparation while we are alive. It is certain we will not have the opportunity to do so after death.

With each incident mentioned previously, all confessing sin, professing belief in Jesus, they were baptized. Infants cannot confess their need for Christ's atoning power.

Baptism of infants was not instituted by Jesus. This practice started until after 200 A.D.

This does not mean that dying infants are lost for eternity. They are totally innocent until they can understand right from wrong. Billy Graham often has used the term "age of accountability". This is what I refer to in the case of an infant. An infant does not yet know sin yet. Sin is an inherited trait of humanity.

When we become aware of sin then we can repent, accept Christ as the eunuch of Ethiopia did, and then baptism.

Chapter 11
Prayer

PRAYER

Prayer is one of the most neglected components of a Christian's life. Its importance and value can never be described by one person in a way that fits every individual. Prayer is invaluable to Christians.

In military basic training in 1962, occasionally an authoritative sounding voice would be heard loudly and distinctly yelling "Hey, you". Those words created an 'instant prayer meeting'. Each trainee hearing those two words instantly prayed, "Oh, God. Please don't let him be yelling at me". Believe me when I say those words were prayed with the *utmost of sincerity*. Many soldiers going into and during combat pray for safety asking God to get them out alive. These prayers are going up as sincerely as any ever spoken. The problem was most forgot the promises made during those moments of stress, personal danger, and great need.

Prayer is far more needful as an everyday, every hour, every minute exercise than when we are facing difficult situations. Apostle Paul instructed the church at Thessalonica in his first letter to them, (5:17) to "Pray without ceasing." He is saying that we should always have a prayerful heart and at every opportunity speak to our Heavenly Father. Prayer is how Christians talk to God. The Bible is how God talks to His people.

In Acts, Chapter 12, we read how Herod had killed James, the brother of John with the sword, then seeing how it

pleased the people arrested Peter with the intention of killing him also after the feast of unleavened bread. While Peter was kept in prison the church prayed without ceasing for him. The results of their continuous prayer was God did miraculously deliver Peter from prison. This shows that prayer is the greatest defensive weapon Christians have. It is also the greatest offensive weapon we have.

Prayer is a great stress reliever, faith builder, barrier remover, and is comforting to a Christian in so many ways.

A few notes about praying.
Gentlemen, remove your hats, caps, or whatever covers your head.

1 Cor 11:4, tells us "*Every man praying or prophesying, having his head covered, dishonoureth his head.*"

When a man prayed he was to have his head uncovered so that he would not dishonor himself and his spiritual head, Jesus Christ. Christ is our head and is also God incarnate and we are created in the image of God and He decided that a man praying with his head covered dishonors Him. Paul writes this while explaining God's appointments in His hierarchy. He says the man is the head of the woman and Christ is the head of the man. Thereby a man praying with his head uncovered brings honor to his head, Jesus Christ.

Prayer is not just for asking of God. It is for thanksgiving from us to Him, shows proper recognition of and to Him, and honors Him.

Has anyone asked you the question "Why do we ask the blessing before we eat?"

The answer is simple. Everything we eat comes either directly or indirectly from the ground. Fruit and vegetables come from the ground. The meat we eat is sustained by the ground. God cursed the ground after Adam and Eve's sin in the Garden of Eden. So when we ask God to bless our food, He does by removing the curse from what we have asked Him to bless. We are to always express our thanks for all He has given and done for us so we thank Him for our food when we ask for Him to bless it.

Prayer is required of a Christian to help their development and spiritual growth. Without it we will never reach the spiritual heights God has intended for us.

Chapter 12
Endurance, Perseverance, And The Will To Win

Endurance, Perseverance, and The Will To Win
James 1:12, Blessed is the man that endureth temptation: for when he is tried, he shall receive the crown of life, which the Lord hath promised to them that love him.
The ESV version reads "Blessed is the man who remains steadfast under trial, for when he has stood the test he will receive the crown of life, which God has promised to those who love him."

Temptations come to Christians in various forms, especially now, as we live in a society that seems to have hit an all-time low in morality. During the 1960s we had the sexual revolution and morality took a hit. In the 1970s and 1980s the decline was much more noticeable as the "coming out of the closet" time came about. Since the 1990s the drug culture has exploded. The devil uses every possible avenue to tempt the Christian. Commercials on television for chewing gum has used, for the last fifty years, sex to sell their products. A young woman in scantily clad swimwear which has gotten smaller over the years. This is to attract customers through lust.

Any party scene on TV usually includes alcoholic beverages and attractive females. Why? Sex sells.

As Christians, we must persevere. I enjoy watching Clint Eastwood western movies.

One of my favorite is "The Outlaw Josey Wales". The old Indian tells Josey that some of his tribe, including him, were taken to Washington D. C. and politicians told them to "endeavor to persevere". I especially like the way the old Indian says those words.

Perseverance is endurance, holding fast, being faithful, never giving up. A great example is given by the Apostle Paul in 2 Corinthians 11, verses 23 to 28:
23 Are they ministers of Christ? (I speak as a fool) I am more; in labours more abundant, in stripes above measure, in prisons more frequent, in deaths oft.
24 Of the Jews five times received I forty stripes save one.
25 Thrice was I beaten with rods, once was I stoned, thrice I suffered shipwreck, a night and a day I have been in the deep;
26 In journeyings often, in perils of waters, in perils of robbers, in perils by mine own countrymen, in perils by the heathen, in perils in the city, in perils in the wilderness, in perils in the sea, in perils among false brethren;
27 In weariness and painfulness, in watchings often, in hunger and thirst, in fastings often, in cold and nakedness.
28 Beside those things that are without, that which cometh upon me daily, the care of all the churches.

Paul endured it all, no matter how bad it was, because he kept in his mind and heart a view of what awaited after life's journey was over.

That, I think, gave him the will to win. He had come too far to look back to what was before accepting Christ. There was nothing that was worth going back to. So he endured, he "endeavored to persevere".

LET'S GO TO HEAVEN

Chapter 13
Clydesdale And A Puppy Dog

Clydesdale and a Puppy Dog
Most everyone has heard of and seen the Clydesdale horses on film. To me they are the most magnificent horses in the world. Being much bigger than most horses makes me feel they are much stronger than the average horse.

I have heard it said numerous times "Life is like a game." In some instances, it may apply. Theodore Roosevelt said the following: "In life, as in a football game, the principle to follow is: hit the line hard."

Our middle son, Bo was a four-sport letterman in high school and thus his concepts of sports he is a very good coach in several sports. I think football is his best sport. Of course, I acknowledge being somewhat bias as his Dad and high school football is my personal favorite of all sports.

Bo has had some players who possessed tremendous athletic skills. The team in the fall of 1999, was loaded with very good athletes. This team had a dynamo as quarterback, Drew Mohr. A lineman who was a natural leader, Bo Meisner. A freshman, Chad Sowers, later an all-state footballer. As a junior he was state champion wrestler. As a senior he moved to a weight class thirty pounds heavier than the previous year, went undefeated all season long but lost the state title match on a very controversial call. This was a remarkable feat. One of my favorite was a coach's dream named Mike Chester. Watching him in one playoff game was like seeing the

biggest Clydesdale furiously attacking a "Heinz 57" puppy dog. In this particular game Mike scored five (5) touchdowns. Though Mike is looked upon as the hero of one particular playoff game there were others who contributed greatly in this game.

The game was between Mohawk and Smithville. A few years later our eldest son, Alvin, did a technology workshop at Smithville School. One of Smithville's staff said: "Trusty, that name sounds familiar". "You are probably thinking of my brother from Mohawk School. He teaches and coaches there". The fellow told of how Mohawk had beaten Smithville. Alvin said that he was at the game with his Dad. The staff member says "..... Yeah, Mohawk had this kid who scored five touchdowns against us.

As it has been a long time and my memory is not nearly what it used to be I don't recall all the plays nor their exact sequence. I spoke with Mike and he and his wife Amy provided me with newspaper clippings of the game. One heading written in large red letters "Chester-field" was obvious because Mike Chester seemed to own the field in that game.

After the game the Smithville coach had nothing but good things to say about Mike. "He's just a great athlete. He did it all. Hands, passing, running. That kid had it all." This makes me think of my all-time favorite college basketball player, Bill Walton. I have a DVD about college greats and Henry Bibby spoke of Walton saying, "Every night you would see something different from Bill. He had the full package." This was and still is my feelings about Mike Chester.

- Here are Mike's stats for that game.
- Scored three rushing touchdowns
- Two receiving TDs
- Carried the ball 28 times for 137 yards
- Was one of two halfback option passes for 45 yards
- Punted twice averaging over 45 yards, one for over 47 yards in the air
- On defense, he intercepted a pass with 34 seconds to go which sealed the win
- WOW, WOW, WOW, and WOW!!

I remember Teddy Roosevelt's quote, "In life, as in a football game, the principle to follow is: hit the line hard." Mike Chester hit everything and everyone hard in that game. He was a joy to watch.

Mike did more than could be asked for in that game. Surely a hero, but there were others who did some great things. During the first half Smithville had a linebacker that was constantly in our backfield often disrupting Mohawk's plays. As defensive coordinator, Bo, took out one lineman and inserted freshman Chad Sauers. Bo told me later that he told Chad his job was to stop that linebacker from crossing the line of scrimmage. "If number 15 gets in our backfield, I'll kick your butt." Number 15 did cross the line of scrimmage a couple times but the play was already working and he was ineffective.

Another running back, Brandon Brause, gained 119 yards on 14 carries. Defenses so keyed on Mike Chester it offered good opportunities for Brandon. At halftime we trailed 21-13, as Mohawk had scored with 57 seconds left.

In the second half Bo's defense put the brakes on Smithville's wing T offense. With less than five and on-half minutes in the game Mohawk finally took the lead on Mike Chester's fourth TD. After that score the other team started a drive of 65 yards. They had not had a first down the entire second half. With 1:16 left they scored to regain the lead. Most of Mohawk's fans had our hearts sink. Bo told me later that he felt that way also. He heard Bo Meisner say "Okay guys, two minute drill. We've done it every day in practice all season long."

Beginning at their 19 yard line, Drew Mohr passes 17 yards to Kevin Kinseed, then the defense swarmed and caught Mike Chester in the backfield for a three yard loss. Coach Jacoby called a halfback option. Having called one earlier in the game when Mike's pass to Drew fell short, the defense was sure it would be another pass to Drew Mohr. When Mike got the ball and Drew rolled out, Mike passed 45 yards to Kevin Kingseed at the 26 yard line. After an incomplete pass Drew placed a perfect pass in Mike's hands, Mike turns and a few steps crosses the goal line, 34.3 seconds left. Smithville passed four times with Mike Chester intercepting the fourth pass as time expired.

Mike Chester could not have won that game without all the plays in which so many teammates did what they were taught to do. Each one doing their job was the

resulted in "Mike the Clydesdale" accomplishing all he did that night in 1999.

As big as the Clydesdales are they can be defeated. I share a story from God's word to support that statement. There are many stories from the Bible to illustrate this.

When God told Gideon his 32,000, men were too many to go against the 135,000, Philistines (or Clydesdales). Following God's instructions Gideon's forces were reduced to 300, who went into battle and had a decisive victory without "firing a shot".

One of my personal favorites is David going against Goliath, with Goliath being the Clydesdale.

Chapter seventeen of First Samuel tells how the Philistines and Israel were encamped on mountains opposite each other with the valley of Elah between them. David, the lad who would later become King of Israel, was sent to take food to his three older brothers who were with King Saul. While there the Philistine giant Goliath came out as he had every morning and evening for some time and challenged Israel to fight by sending out their best fighter. Whichever one won, their country would rule over the other. This infuriated David when he saw the men of Israel scared to face this man. He asked the men around him, "What shall be done to the man that killeth this Philistine, and taketh away the reproach from Israel? for who is this uncircumcised Philistine, that he should defy the armies of the living God?" His oldest brother Eliab was irritated by David's question and let him know it.

Word of what David said made it to King Saul, so the king sent for him. When Saul seen David and realizes he is but a young boy his reaction is "you can't go against Goliath". The giant was six cubits and a span tall. A span was about six inches, and a cubit was the distance from the elbow and the fingertip which varied between eighteen and twenty-two inches. This makes Goliath between nine and a half and eleven and a half feet tall. Who wouldn't be scared of such a formidable opponent? Anyone with common sense.

David tells the king that while tending his father's sheep a bear and a lion took sheep and he gave pursuit of each and killed them and retrieved the sheep. This causes the king to rethink and reevaluate the boy. "This boy is one tough cookie" is what I would be thinking. The boy tells the king that as the Lord had delivered from the lion and bear and would deliver him from the Philistine. It impresses me that David referred to Goliath as "the Philistine" and not as "the giant". He has confidence that his God will give him victory. King Saul puts his armor on David. When Saul was made king the Bible makes note of him being much taller than most people so I think of how much too large the king's battle gear is for David. He tells the king he can't us this battle gear. He puts it off, goes out to meet Goliath who mocks him and probably had all the confidence in the world that he would tear this boy limb from limb.

Reading this story, I notice the confidence of the Giant, but also the scorn for David and all God's people. He is certain he will win. He is possibly thinking of David as a, "pip-squeak" if they used that term then.

However, the "pip-squeak" comes to meet him with a different attitude. David could be thinking "You have insulted the God of my people by your actions and words. That calls for punishment. My God will give you into my hand now."

Goliath *thinks* he is the Clydesdale when he sees David's smallness of size.

However, with David's faith in God's abilities and power, he *knows* he is the Clydesdale.

David tells the giant: *"Thou comest to me with a sword, and with a spear, and with a shield: but I come to thee in the name of the Lord of hosts, the God of the armies of Israel, whom thou hast defied.*

This day will the Lord deliver thee into mine hand; and I will smite thee, and take thine head from thee; and I will give the carcasses of the host of the Philistines this day unto the fowls of the air, and to the wild beasts of the earth; that all the earth may know that there is a God in Israel."

David had taken the weapon he was most accurate with, his sling, to face Goliath. His ammo was five smooth stones. He would only need one of the stones but had ample for the job. His sling hit the only vulnerable place the giant had, his forehead. The giant fell, David goes over to him, stands upon him, and David having no sword in his hand, draws the giant's sword and removes Goliath's head. This caused all the other Philistines to flee for their lives. Israel had won by miraculous means.

Mike Chester and the 1999 Mohawk football team were not expected to win the game against Smithville. Being united, as one, Mike was made to look like a Clydesdale, though I'm confident he never thought of himself in that manner. David, through his faith in Israel's God, made the Philistines look as a huge number of small puppies scared and in full panic.

Chapter 14
Things Change

Things Change

I was born December 19, 1944, in a small place called Lackey, KY. This was during the "Battle of the Bulge" of World War II. The sign entering Lackey said "POP 300", referring to the population. The same sign was there in 2015, the last time I was there. Time spent there prior to being transplanted in Ohio was happiness, fond memories and good times. The animals we had were like most others there. My dog, Curly, a shepherd, was a brother to Granddaddy's dog Brownie. Curly and I would climb the hills all around our house, play together, and were best friends.

Labor Day weekend 1951, we move to Ohio. I hated it here. Everybody talked funny. Had I an inkling how to get back to Lackey I would have taken off on foot to get there.

How things have changed. Though we visited Lackey every summer until I finished high school and enjoying friends there, it didn't seem to change. A visit in 1971, I noticed changes. Most of the people I knew either passed on or moved.

Across from the old Three Way Inn is so grown up I can't tell if the old swinging bridge is still there. No longer can I see the hill across the bottom from the swinging bridge and the railroad track where my goat "Billie" would charge the train every time it moved as the tipple loaded the cars with coal. Billie would come tearing off the hill, hit the coal car's wheels, bounce off, hit the wheels again,

with the same effect, then come back up the hill to the house until the cars made the moving sound again.

Age has taken a toll on me and I can no longer climb the hills as before. This tells me my time left on earth has diminished something fierce and I'm closer to the end. Since I don't know just when or what date my leaving will be, I want to live each day as though it might be the day.

For many years, I have searched, via the internet, many subjects. One subject is the last words people spoke.
Thomas Edison said "It is very beautiful over there".
Mother Teresa, "Jesus, I love you, Jesus, I love you".
Thomas Cranmer, Archbishop of Canterbury, "I see Heaven open and Jesus on the right hand of God".

This was similar with what the best deacon God had at the Jerusalem Church, Stephen, after telling the church leaders how misguided they were in Acts 7:54-60:
When they heard these things, they were cut to the heart, and they gnashed on him with their teeth.
55 But he, being full of the Holy Ghost, looked up stedfastly into heaven, and saw the glory of God, and Jesus standing on the right hand of God,
56 And said, Behold, I see the heavens opened, and the Son of man standing on the right hand of God.
57 Then they cried out with a loud voice, and stopped their ears, and ran upon him with one accord,
58 And cast him out of the city, and stoned him: and the witnesses laid down their clothes at a young man's feet, whose name was Saul.
59 And they stoned Stephen, calling upon God, and saying, Lord Jesus, receive my spirit.

60 And he kneeled down, and cried with a loud voice, Lord, lay not this sin to their charge. And when he had said this, he fell asleep.

My wish is to be with others who know Jesus and be able to see God's messengers coming. I might say.

Let's Go to Heaven!

Chapter 15
Old Testament Feast Days

Old Testament Feast Days
Every religion seems to have its holy days and seasons. Since the Jewish nation was God's chosen, covenant people. He made covenants and gave these feast days to them. Each feast is observed at a particular time, and as well, for a particular reason.

This gives believers the opportunity to express with joy how thankful we are to Him who gives us everything. There are seven Feasts, with all of them being based on the Jewish Lunar calendar. All seven of the Feasts relate to Israel's agricultural seasons. These seasons were both Spring and Fall.

Each Feast signifies something about Jesus and His coming to earth to redeem lost humanity. The first Feast was Passover, signifies Jesus at Calvary. The Passover, when instituted in the Old Testament, shows how the blood of the sacrificed lamb being placed on the door of each home, spared those within it from death.

This relates to Jesus at Calvary shedding His blood so humanity would be spared an eternal death. His blood paid the debt each person owes to God because of the sins we have committed. Jesus was the ***perfect sacrifice*** that was demanded. All who believe in what Jesus death accomplished at Calvary simply must confess 'I believe in and accept what Jesus did for me by His death".

To cite what Paul wrote in his epistle to the Romans Chapter ten

"Rom 10:1 Brethren, my heart's desire and prayer to God for Israel is, that they might be saved.
2 For I bear them record that they have a zeal of God, but not according to knowledge.
3 For they being ignorant of God's righteousness, and going about to establish their own righteousness, have not submitted themselves unto the righteousness of God.
4 For Christ is the end of the law for righteousness to every one that believeth.
5 For Moses describeth the righteousness which is of the law, That the man which doeth those things shall live by them.
6 But the righteousness which is of faith speaketh on this wise, Say not in thine heart, Who shall ascend into heaven? (that is, to bring Christ down from above:)
7 Or, Who shall descend into the deep? (that is, to bring up Christ again from the dead.)
8 The word is nigh thee, even in thy mouth, and in thy heart: that is, the word of faith, which we preach;
9 That if thou shalt confess with thy mouth the Lord Jesus, and shalt believe in thine heart that God hath raised him from the dead, thou shalt be saved.
10 For with the heart man believeth unto righteousness; and with the mouth confession is made unto salvation.
11 For the scripture saith, Whosoever believeth on him shall not be ashamed."

Paul states that Christ is the end of the Law for righteousness. The Law was given as a temporary guidance until the Messiah would come and establish the plan of salvation. Jesus death on the cross which Jesus did by His love, fulfilled the Law. Love fulfilled the Law so now righteousness comes by faith, faith in what Jesus accomplished at Calvary.

All the Feasts were built upon the foundation of Passover.

The Feast of Unleavened Bread, started one day after Passover, lasted seven days.

The Feast of the Firstfruits started on the second day of the Feast of Unleavened Bread. With the barley harvest is beginning to ripen. The first sheaf of it is cut and presented to the Lord. God's acceptance of it was a pledge to Israel of a full harvest.

The feasts coming in the Fall of the year:
Feast of Trumpets - called Rosh Hashanah - means "Head of Year". Blowing of the trumpet in Israel was a call to a solemn assembly or when God sent Israel to war.
Feast of Trumpets depicts the return of Jesus to rapture the church and judge the wicked.
Feast of Passover refers to the death of Messiah as sacrificial and substitutionary (in our place).
The feast of Unleavened Bread indicated the Messiah's body would not rot in the grave.
The Feast of Firstfruits began on the second day of the seven day Feast of Unleavened Bread.
Feast of Weeks was to last 49, days. The day after made it fifty days after Feast of Firstfruits. This feast was also called Pentecost. Pentecost simply means fiftieth.

The Day of Atonement came nine days after the Feast of Trumpets. The time period between these feasts is known as "the days of awe."

Many scholars believe that on the Day of Atonement the Church will be raptured and God will begin to pour out His wrath upon the inhabitants of the earth.

The Feast of Tabernacles usually occurs in October. Many Jews put up huts or booths made of bulrushes to remind them of the temporary housing the Israelites had on their forty-year journey from Egypt to Canaan.

The Feast of Tabernacles denotes a new beginning in a place of peace.

Passover – redemption.
Unleavened Bread– sanctification.
Firstfruits – resurrection.
Weeks – organization.
Trumpets – Jesus return to get the Church, His bride.
*Atonemen*t – also called Yom Kippur – refers to a day when Israel repents of her sins and turns to Jesus for forgiveness.
Tabernacles – when Jesus sets up his rule among men.

These Feast days keep reminding us of past events connected to Christianity.

They should stir our hearts to desire more knowledge of the reasons for which they are sacred. It should create a desire to understand the mysteries which can be learned from each of these special days.

As we are in a covenant relation with God, initiated by Him, we no longer are separated from Him who gives us true life and happiness.

The first thought of the annual Jewish festivals is that of joy and being thankful for the many bounties that we receive from Him.

The first gift that God gave man was daily sustenance provided for him. God made Adam from dust, afterward making Eve from one of Adam's ribs. He then placed them in the Garden of Eden which had everything they would ever need for food. For all God has given us we should ever be thankful and always express to Him our gratitude.

Three great annual festivals, Passover, Pentecost, and the Feast of Tabernacles, were days of thanksgiving for the fruits of the earth given by God to man.

Since the Bible does not give many details about Heaven, the studying of these feast days has thrilled my soul deeply. It has caused me to pause and reflect on what I think Heaven will be more like.

Chapter 16
Why Is There A Rooster?

Why Is There A Rooster? Matthew 26:31-35

As a young boy in KY., I lived a very happy life. We had chickens, hogs, a milk cow, a Billy- goat, cats and a faithful dog. When we lived on the hillside above the railroad next to the bottom going to the swinging bridge which was across the road from what was then the 3Way Inn, each morning I heard the rooster crow. I never gave much thought about it other than the older folks were up before the rooster sounded out the first time. I had formed the brilliant opinion, as a four year old, that "Mr. Rooster" crowed to wake up us *young'uns.*

What purpose does a rooster serve?
Definition of:

- A rooster, also known as a cockerel or cock, is a male bird, usually a male chicken.
- Mature male chickens less than one year old are called cockerels.
- The term "rooster" originates in the United States, and the term is widely used throughout North America, as well as Australia and New Zealand.

"Roosting" is the action of perching aloft to sleep at day, which is done by both sexes. The rooster is polygamous, but cannot guard several nests of eggs at once. He guards the general area where his hens are nesting, and attacks other roosters that enter his territory. During the daytime, a rooster often sits on a high perch, usually 3 to

5 feet off the ground, to serve as a lookout for his group (hence the term "rooster"). He sounds a distinctive alarm call if predators are nearby.

The rooster is often portrayed as crowing at the break of dawn ("cock-a-doodle-doo"). However, while many roosters crow shortly after waking up, this idea is not exactly true. A rooster can and will crow at any time of the day. Some roosters are especially vociferous, crowing almost constantly, while others only crow a few times a day. These differences are dependent both upon the rooster's breed and individual personality. A rooster can often be seen sitting on fence posts or other objects, where he crows to proclaim his territory.

Roosters have several other calls as well, and can cluck, similar to the hen. Roosters occasionally make a patterned series of clucks to attract hens to a source of food, the same way a mother hen does for her chicks

Learning this, I surmise the "cock-a-doodle-doo" sound isn't to awaken the young'uns.
It is an alarm to make the other roosters know "I'm here, I'm awake, I'm watching over what is mine."

Jesus in the Garden of Gethsemane
John 18:10 – Then Simon Peter having a sword drew it, and smote the high priest's servant, and cut off his right ear. The servant's name was Malchus.

Peter had promised that he would die for Jesus and he might have thought he could save Jesus or at least go down fighting. He was better at fishing than swinging a sword.

He, I think tried to hit the head of the high priest's servant Malchus not just his ear. Luke wrote that Jesus healed the man's ear (Luke 22:51), showing love for His enemies!

Peter's blind loyalty missed God's plan. Zeal without knowledge in religion often leads men astray (Rom 10:2). "... they have a zeal of God, but not according knowledge ...".

"Peter was so carried away by the fervor of his zeal and love for Christ, that he regarded neither the weakness of his own flesh nor the truth of his Master's word."

Jesus tells Peter to put his sword up.
By this he is not teaching that we should not defend ourselves as well as other Christians.

He is simply telling Peter to not interfere with God's plan, which Peter did not know all.

Later Jesus made the statement that He could call 12 legions of angels ... but His mission would not be accomplished.

After Jesus was arrested in Gethsemane, He was led by the soldiers to Caiaphas, the high priest. But first there was a brief trial before the former high priest, Annas, who was Caiaphas' father-in-law. That delaying tactic apparently gave Caiaphas time to assemble the "Sanhedrin" quickly.

Peter followed the Lord at a distance and came into the courtyard of the high priest's home to await the outcome. While Jesus was undergoing His trial before the Sanhedrin, Peter was also undergoing a testing. He had

followed the Lord and gained entrance into the house of the high priest. As he sat in the courtyard awaiting the outcome of the trial, he had three opportunities to speak up for his Lord. All three times he denied he ever knew the Accused or was in any way ever connected with Him. ***The first denial*** occurred when a servant girl said in front of the others that he was one of those who had been with Jesus.

Another girl at the gate of the courtyard more directly pointed Peter out as one who had indeed been with Jesus.

Finally, a number of those present came and accused Peter of being one who had been with Jesus for his Galilean accent gave him away.

With the third accusation, Peter began to call down curses on himself and he swore. The calling of curses on himself was a legal way of seeking to affirm one's innocence; if the calamities did not follow, he would be assumed innocent.

One of the menial servants who attended to the outer door of the court, says: *"Thou wast also with the Nazarene, even Jesus. But he denied, saying, I neither know, nor understand what thou sayest."* This shows the great terror of Peter, He was intimidated by the question of a poor servant-girl. He denied his Lord; *"I neither know, nor understand what thou sayest.* Every word here is emphatic.

Afterwards when he had received the Holy Spirit, Peter said, 'We ought to obey God rather than man.' He had learned a lesson through heartbreak.

As he publicly denied his Lord the third time, immediately a rooster crowed.
That triggered in his thinking the words of the Lord, Before the rooster crows, you will deny Me three times.

Peter knew immediately he had failed the Lord. Though he had affirmed that he would never forsake the Lord, he had publicly denied the One he loved. Filled with remorse, he left the courtyard and wept bitterly. His tears were tears of true repentance for having forsaken and denied the Lord.

This one rooster justifies all roosters who have awoken you in the wee hours of the morning, those who seem never to shut up by crowing all through the day, and those who strut like they are hot stuff.

His "cock-a-doodle-doo" was to Peter as good as any sermon he had heard Jesus give.

Remember what the rooster says to the other ones: "I'm here, I'm awake, I'm watching over what is mine."

This feathered fellow in essence preached a sermon to Peter.
Subject: Remembrance
Peter immediately remembered the words of Jesus just hours earlier. **You will deny me thrice.**

The rooster told Peter "When Jesus tells you something BELIEVE IT. It will be as He speaks.

Never contradict what the Lord says. He knows more than we do. We are not to be so self- assured in what we think. We may not always do what we think we will.

Every time Jesus says something you immediately respond by saying something stupid. From now on take in what He says long enough to understand it.
Then you won't be sticking your foot in your mouth all the time.

The rooster is saying, "Peter, get a grip on yourself".
Peter didn't recall or rely on what he had seen Jesus do.

The Effect the Sermon Had on Peter
Immediately he was heartbroken: He went out & wept bitterly. Broken hearts can only come to Jesus for true repentance.

How long did this message impact Peter?
The remainder of his life.

1 Peter 1:1 Peter, an apostle of Jesus Christ, to the strangers scattered throughout Pontus, Galatia, Cappadocia, Asia, and Bithynia,
2 Elect according to the foreknowledge of God the Father, through sanctification of the Spirit, unto obedience and sprinkling of the blood of Jesus Christ: Grace unto you, and peace, be multiplied.
3 Blessed be the God and Father of our Lord Jesus Christ, which according to his abundant mercy hath begotten us again unto a lively hope by the resurrection of Jesus Christ from the dead,
4 To an inheritance incorruptible, and undefiled, and that fadeth not away, reserved in heaven for you,
5 Who are kept by the power of God through faith unto salvation ready to be revealed in the last time.

1 Peter 2:1 Therefore laying aside all malice, and all guile, and hypocrisies, and envies, and all evil speakings,

2 As newborn babes, desire the sincere milk of the word, that ye may grow thereby:
3 If so be ye have tasted that the Lord is gracious.

Peter, in Acts Chapter 2, gave them a complete discourse on religious education.

This, seasoned by the Holy Spirit, touched hearts so strongly that 3,000, people accepted Jesus on the spot.
I give the rooster credit for all the good Peter did for Jesus in his lifetime.

He still wasn't a perfect man; but knew how to repent.

Chapter 17
How Much Is Your Preacher Worth?

How much is your preacher worth?

Paul writing to his "son in the faith" Timothy, answered this question for us.
1 Tim 5:17 Let the elders that rule well be counted worthy of double honour, especially they who labour in the word and doctrine.
18 For the scripture saith, Thou shalt not muzzle the ox that treadeth out the corn. And, The labourer is worthy of his reward.

The presbytery hold positions of leadership in the church and direct the affairs of that church. Elders have the oversight of the affairs of the congregation. For this they received pay; but those who excelled in this ministry of leadership were to be considered worthy of double honor, or twice the amount as the rest. Preachers care for the needs of a congregation far beyond the preaching and teaching. These duties are primary to the ministry and are of most importance.

Teaching this, yet in 1 Corinthians nine, verses fifteen through twenty-three, Paul reserved the right not to receive support from a congregation which countless men have done through the centuries.

In verse seventeen above Paul speaks of counting them worthy of double honor. For many pastors, just being appreciated by our congregations is sufficient.

While attending the Athletes In Action Super Bowl Breakfast the last week of January 1993, I was privileged to hear Christian testimonies from NFL athletes. Bart Starr was the emcee, Tom Landry was the speaker, Tommy Aggie, backup for Emmett Smith, and Frank Reich, who was backup for Jim Kelly of the Bills for nine seasons, each spoke briefly.

In the Conference Wild Card game Jim Kelly went down to injury. In the second half the Bills were down by 35 to 3. Frank Reich took over and brought the Bills back to win in overtime. The greatest come back in NFL history until this past Super Bowl.

What he said at the breakfast has brought me great thoughts since then. His words "I don't want to be remembered as a football player who was a Christian. I want to be remembered as a Christian who just happened to play football." He had his priorities in order.

My desire is to be remembered as a Christian who served Him honorably, explored and taught the depths of God's Word, and anxiously waited for His coming. If I die prior to His return, I will be happy and at peace. As David said and was quoted in
Acts 2:25-28 *For David speaketh concerning him, I foresaw the Lord always before my face, for he is on my right hand, that I should not be moved:*
26 Therefore did my heart rejoice, and my tongue was glad; moreover also my flesh shall rest in hope:
27 Because thou wilt not leave my soul in hell, neither wilt thou suffer thine Holy One to see corruption.
28 Thou hast made known to me the ways of life; thou shalt make me full of joy with thy countenance.

Job spoke of the grave as a time appointed by God.
Job 14:10-15, But man dieth, and wasteth away: yea, man giveth up the ghost, and where is he? 11 As the waters fail from the sea, and the flood decayeth and drieth up: 12 So man lieth down, and riseth not: till the heavens be no more, they shall not awake, nor be raised out of their sleep. 13 O that thou wouldest hide me in the grave, that thou wouldest keep me secret, until thy wrath be past, that thou wouldest appoint me a set time, and remember me! 14 If a man die, shall he live again? all the days of my appointed time will I wait, till my change come. 15 Thou shalt call, and I will answer thee: thou wilt have a desire to the work of thine

Chapter 18
Judgment

Judgment

Be happy to the point of being thrilled that the judgments of people on earth are often wrong when they make a decision about others. The Bible tells us to "use a righteous judgment" when judging others. Not knowing all the facts will often cause people to judge inappropriately.

I would never want to be a judge in any contest. Whether it be singing, playing a musical instrument, a sport which I don't know thoroughly. My uncle Troy of Wabash, Indiana during the early 1960s, worked with a man named Jr. Webb. He told Troy that he had a sister trying to make it in Country Music. "She's made a 45 record and if you want I'll bring it over to your house and you can listen to it." Jr. brought the record over and Troy played it on his record player. After listening to it Jr. asked "What do you think?" One thing I always admired about my uncle Troy was his straightforwardness. His answer was, "She'll never make it". I don't know how Jr. felt about my uncle's opinion. He had asked and was told. I can imagine when Jr. finally realized Troy was incorrect in his prediction. Troy's answer of his honest opinion never bothered their friendship, as should be. Guess who Jr.'s sister was. You might even have heard of her or even listened to her on radio, or possibly watched her on television, or perhaps you saw a movie about her called "Coal Miner's Daughter". Loretta Lynn did well for herself in country music.

Opinions and judgments of people can so easily be wrong. I used to be a fan of O.J. Simpson. When he was charged with murder I was shocked. I watched portions of the trial and thinking he may really have done it. However, when Johnny Cochran said in his summation, referring to when the prosecution asked the Juice to try on the gloves, "If it doesn't fit you must acquit", I was impressed and felt the jury would give the verdict they rendered. I wished all along he had not committed the crime, yet was not sure the jury got it right.

Years later I read Mark Fuhrman's book "Murder in Brentwood" and the book "Outrage" by Vincent Bugliosi, the District Attorney who prosecuted Charles Manson, and then was convinced that O.J. was guilty. The book "Outrage" pointed out so many things the prosecutor's office failed to present as evidence that would have rendered a different verdict. Still, I could be wrong.

There is a day already appointed for a judgment of every person that lived on this earth. Recorded in Acts *17:30 And the times of this ignorance God winked at; but now commandeth all men every where to repent:*
31 Because he hath appointed a day, in the which he will judge the world in righteousness by that man whom he hath ordained; whereof he hath given assurance unto all men, in that he hath raised him from the dead.

This day will reveal all personal secrets, each thing we have hidden, nothing will be left covered or hidden from the One who will be the Judge on that day.

No excuses will be allowed. We will have no one to blame, only ourselves. We cannot point to what someone else did to get sympathy. It will be the saddest day many ever

experienced. However, it will only get worse when we are instructed to leave Christ's presence, for we will be cast into a lake of fire that will never be extinguished.

Because I knew this as a teenager, I made preparation to avoid hearing Jesus say "Depart". I am prayed up, dressed up, having His blood applied to my heart, ready, and waiting with a looking forward to hearing Him say, "Enter in".

Therefore, we need to establish a personal relationship with Jesus Christ ......NOW!

Chapter 19
Amazing Grace

Amazing Grace
The song "Amazing Grace" was written by John Newton, captain of a slave trade ship. On a voyage through a violent storm, thinking the ship would sink, he spoke the words "Lord, have mercy on us", and the storm passed. Remembering the words he had spoken, he felt God had intervened on his behalf. He believed in God.

Influenced by two great preachers which he became acquainted with, George Whitefield and John Wesley, he entered the ministry.

Amazing grace! (How sweet the sound)
– That saved a wretch like me!
I once was lost, but now am found,
-- Was blind, but now I see.
Twas grace that taught my heart to fear,
-- And grace my fears relieved;
How precious did that grace appear,
-- The hour I first believed!
Thro' many dangers, toils and snares,
-- I have already come;
Tis grace has brought me safe thus far,
-- And grace will lead me home.
The Lord has promised good to me,
-- His word my hope secures;
He will my shield and portion be,
-- As long as life endures.
Yes, when this flesh and heart shall fail,
-- And mortal life shall cease;

I shall possess, within the veil,
-- A life of joy and peace.
The earth shall soon dissolve like snow,
-- The sun forbear to shine;
But God, who called me here below,
-- Will be forever mine.

This song has been sung since the 1700s, and has never gotten old or out dated. When a person personally accepts Jesus Christ as their Savior the words become very real in our lives.

God's Grace truly is amazing.
Someone asked this years ago. "How can a brown cow eat green grass still give white milk? I cannot explain the science of that question. However, there is one similar where science isn't involved. How can the red blood of Jesus Christ cleanse every stain of sin?

The answer is that a perfect sacrifice was required. And Jesus was perfect, the only perfect person ever on earth. Since Jesus is perfect, let's see the words of the prophet Isaiah.
Isa 1:18 Come now, and let us reason together, saith the Lord: though your sins be as scarlet, they shall be as white as snow; though they be red like crimson, they shall be as wool.

When I was living in sin I felt filthy, rotten, guilty, useless, not worth anything. There were people I loved and I knew loved me. But something was missing.

When I invited Jesus into my life I felt clean, pure, the guilt was gone. I felt new. Later I understood why I felt new. I was new.

2 Cor 5:17 states "Therefore if any man be in Christ, he is a new creature: old things are passed away; behold, all things are become new."

What Makes God's Grace So Special?
The way he transforms lives. He changes hearts, removing hatred, changes minds by putting love in our hearts.

Having lost my Dad when I was only ten years old, I didn't have the honor to get to know him as a man and have the relationship with him as I have with our three sons. Many of the things I currently know about him were told to me by my mother and Dad's youngest brother. Dad was a real scoundrel before accepting Jesus into his life. So much so, that the people in Lackey, KY., where we lived were taking bets on how long Dad would be true to Christ. The bets ranged from two weeks to six months. But the change Jesus made was so profound it lasted the remainder of his life.

Chapter 20
I Met A Man

I Met A Man

I met a man I could never forget.
I was but seventeen, just graduated high school, joined the United States Air Force.
Twelve days after arriving at Homestead Air Force Base, Florida, the Cuban Missile Crisis began.
During this time, I met Robert D. Blair. He had returned to the States from Hahn Air Base, Germany.

My first impression of him never changed in all the years since the Missile Crisis in 1962.
His friendliness and smile set him apart from most of the other GIs.
Something between us just clicked. We became friends instantly.

Bob was a Chess player and wanted to teach me the game; but I wasn't interested. Probably there was so much to absorb at one time. In 1975, a friend in my hometown taught me and I truly loved the game. Someone Bob had been stationed with in Germany played Chess with Bob by mail. He would get a letter from him, go to his room, get his chess set out, set up the board, and concentrate. And concentrate, and concentrate, and I would go do something else.

Bob had a car and would let me to use it to go to a Free Will Baptist Church in Miami, Florida. He refused to go with me but was nice enough to loan me his car. For that

I was thankful at the time. After we reconnected I felt indebted because of it.

In February 1964, Bob was transferred to Clark Air Base, Philippine Islands.

In early 1965, I had applied to cross train to another AFSC/MOS. Captain Joseph Martin asked me to come work for him in public information. Every time someone new transferred in they were to clear in through our office. A GI came from Clark and I asked if he knew Robert Blair or Dennis Stanley who shipped with Bob to Clark. I was told Stanley was working in Confinement (what the Army calls the Stockade) and Bob was a prisoner. My thoughts were "What went wrong? Stanley was more apt to be locked up than Bob". When Bob and I reconnected I relayed this story and he laughed as he explained what happened. He had loaned his car to a guy and the fellow robbed a place and they got the license number and arrested Bob. It took a few days to prove Bob had nothing to do with it.

Bob and I reconnected through the web site vetfriends.com. After signing up on the site I would go back every couple weeks, and finally saw "Retired Master Sgt. Robert D. Blair. I left a message and the next week I received an e-mail from him with his phone number. In his message he said, "I've checked you out, and you are a Free Will Baptist preacher. I got saved and attend a Free Will Baptist Church."

I called him immediately. We had a long talk about our families, the places he was stationed, and how good it was to connect again. During this first conversation Bob told me that I was one person he could never get out of

his mind. I told him he was often on my mind and I prayed for him over the years when I thought about him.

All those years went by and Bob met a man also. The very man I had always wanted him to meet. That man was Jesus Christ, the Saviour of the world. Bob certainly enjoyed his relationship with the Lord.

Bob arranged for me to come to Shady Nook Free Will Baptist Church and have the great honor to preach last June. An experience I will always cherish in my memory. Before leaving we shook hands and I gave Bob a hug, telling him that "we may never see each other here again but I promise to meet you in Heaven."

Speaking with Carolyn, Bob's wife, she said "He's up there having all that fun without me."

We shall meet again. I encourage all Bob's family and friends to accept Jesus so you can say "I'll meet you again, Bob.

LET'S GO TO HEAVEN!

I do now dedicate this book to Robert D. Blair. Though I served with several men whom I have seen since my service ended none were as close to me while I was in the military. Working together, we had good discussions often. Our friendship and respect for each other grew to the point of being unforgettable.

Others I reconnected with: Terry J. Baggott from Nashville, TN., Larry L. Slone, of Winchester, KY, area, and Robert L. Partin of Corbin, KY. All are true friends now as they were then.

Bob Blair was, in his own words, "One person I never forgot", thought of often, prayed for often and now has given me another reason to say: LET'S GO TO HEAVEN

Saying good-by down here is a temporary thing. Our meeting again will be an eternal thing. Until we meet I will hold your memory precious and long for our reunion when Jesus comes.

Bob Blair and family

www.ingramcontent.com/pod-product-compliance
Lightning Source LLC
Chambersburg PA
CBHW060952040426
42445CB00011B/1125
9781940609577